WHERE TO EAT IN KENT

AN INFORMATIVE GUIDE TO

Editor: Alison Moore
Studio co-ordination: Michelle Power, Naomi Davis
Compilation: Mervyn Woodward

CONTENTS

Foreword 3
Where to Eat in Kent 5
Restaurant of the Year 59
Chef's Choice 60
Alphabetical Index to Establishments 62
Alphabetical Index to Towns and Villages 64

Cover Photograph: Eastwell Manor, Boughton Aluph, Ashford

Published by Kingsclere Publications Ltd.
Highfield House, 2 Highfield Avenue, Newbury, Berkshire RG14 5DS

Printed by Warwick Printing Co Ltd at Theatre Street, Warwick CV34 4DR
and
at 112 Bermondsey Street, London SE1 3TX. Tel: 071-378 1579

Extreme care is taken to ensure the accuracy of entries, but neither the Editor nor the Publishers accept any liability for errors, omissions or other mistakes, or any consequences arising therefrom.
All prices correct at time of going to press.

ISBN O 86204 197 X

FOREWORD

Mervyn Woodward

FOREWORD

by Mervyn Woodward

Dining out in good company is one of the great pleasures in life. In this county alone there is a huge variety of choice. A choice of inn, restaurant or hotel; a choice of style of cuisine; a choice of wine – so much and so delightful.

So, who needs a Where to Eat guide? The answer is everyone! At a time when inns are being sold off by the major breweries, hotels are closing and restaurants are failing, you really need an up-to-date idea of where to go. You also need to know what you are likely to be charged, what the establishments have to offer, and where you will find value for money. By being selective, you will help the really good establishments survive – and hopefully speed the demise of the second-rate ones.

There are now many places that charge as much as they can for the least they can get away with. All the places in this guide have been carefully chosen, personally visited and found to be worthy of recommendation to *your* choice.

Some have been in the guide for many years. May they continue to succeed, and may you continue to enjoy them.

Mervyn Woodward
Compiler

To whet your appetite for eating out in

KENT

here is a selection of establishments shown in colour

THE MOUNT EDGCUMBE HOUSE HOTEL

The Common, Tunbridge Wells.
Tel: (0892) 26823

The Mount Edgcumbe is acknowledged to be one of the most interesting restaurants in all of Kent. It comprises several restaurants all under one roof, ranging from the bistro-type atmosphere of La Galoche (a fascinating cellar grotto) to the airy and elegant atmosphere of the main restaurant, which overlooks the common. The à la carte selection changes daily in order to take advantage of the best of seasonal game, fish, meat and poultry, but the first class reputation of the hotel is built upon the wealth of seafood offered, which features oysters, clams, fresh lobster, crab, giant prawns, crayfish and sardines. Vegetarians are catered for and The Mount Edgcumbe was also voted the restaurant with the best cheeseboard in the county, in a competition organised on behalf of the Swiss trade Centre (the panel of judges included Anton Mosimann). The selection is very reasonably priced at £3, inviting guests to become gourmands as well as gourmets.

Centre of Tunbridge Wells

Lunch
Dinner

À la carte £8 – £17
Snacks from £3
House wine £6 per bottle; £1.20 per glass

Vegetarian dishes

Accommodation

Access, Visa

Centre of Tunbridge Wells

Morning coffee
Lunch
Dinner
Bar snacks

À la carte £15 – £20
Lunch from £5
Bar snacks from £2
House wine £6.95

THE BARN

Lonsdale Gardens, Tunbridge Wells,
Tel: (0892) 510424

Very much the focal point in this lovely town, The Barn is ideally situated when you want to take a break from shopping for morning coffee or lunch. The Barn is open for lunch and dinner every day, and is also the ideal venue for private parties and functions of every description. There are two restaurants within the building, plus a delightful terrace, and the selection of fare is varied and imaginative. There are daily specials as well as menu selections, and the home-made soups such as potato and watercress, French onion and crab bisque, to be found amongst the starters, are highly regarded. The à la carte offers such delights as filet de boeuf en croûte, chateaubriand (for two), rack of lamb, filet de porc Normandie and caneton Marco Polo. There is everything from a light snack to a gourmet feast, together with a wide selection of wines from around the world.

THE BARN

LONSDALE GARDENS, TUNBRIDGE WELLS

THE ROSE AND CROWN

High Street, Tonbridge.
Tel: (0732) 357966

The 18th century Rose and Crown, set in Tonbridge's High Street and just across the road from the castle, is one of the highly-esteemed Trusthouse Forte hotels. It offers all the amenities one associates with the group, with three function rooms (which can cater for any event from a small dinner party to a full scale wedding reception). The Chaucer Restaurant concentrates on offering value for money from an imaginative and generous menu. From a selection of eight starters guests might choose barley kidneys (lambs' kidneys served with mushrooms and shallots and cooked in sherry and barley wine) and Friar's spiced chicken. Main courses again show originality, with dishes such as Parson's lamb, Trawlerman's net or hickory chicken. There are also a number of interesting specialities with, for example, Chaucer's Wheel (for two), Poacher's Pouch and Yeoman's Sword.

Centre of Tonbridge

Lunch
Dinner

À la carte £10 – £14
House wine £6.45 per bottle

Vegetarian dishes

Conference facilities

Access, Visa, Amex, Diner's Club

THE ROSE AND CROWN

Centre of Aylesford

Lunch
Dinner

À la carte £26
House wine from £7.90

Conservatory and outdoor dining

Access, Visa, Amex, Diner's Club

THE HENGIST

7/9 High Street, Aylesford, Maidstone.
Tel: (0622) 719273; Fax: (0622) 715027

Named after the first Saxon king of Kent, this incomparable restaurant has established itself over the years with a fine reputation. Not only is The Hengist featured in the major food guides, but it has won the Clean Food Award each year. Everything about The Hengist is imaginative and original. The different courses have been given such names as 'Initial Skirmish', 'Main Battle' and 'Final Surrender'. *Al fresco* dining is available in summer, as the lovely conservatory opens out onto a high terrace patio, and there is superb, if limited, accommodation. The menu includes starters such as mushrooms in garlic and filo pastry, smoked goose breast with Oxford sauce and melon and grape in port. Roast duck with spicy orange sauce; steak, oyster and wild mushrooms pie; veal cutlet with Parma ham; shark fillet with tarragon and fricassée of seafood with spicy lime are a few examples of the type of superb gourmet fare you can expect.

THE HENGIST

7/9 High Street,
Aylesford,
Near Maidstone.
Tel (0622) 719273
Fax (0622) 715027

"A corner of the conservatory for pre-dinner drinks."

THE DOG AND BEAR HOTEL

The Square, Lenham, near Maidstone.
Tel: (0622) 858219

This delightful old coaching inn dates from 1602 and is one of Shepherd Neame's superb Invicta country inns. Queen Anne visited the inn in 1704 and the royal coat of arms is displayed above the main entrance. Although the hotel may look much as it did all those years ago, it is now refurbished to the highest standards and has 25 lovely bedrooms, all *en suite*, with colour TV, direct dial telephones, trouser press and shoe polishers. The hotel offers a same day laundry service. The food is traditional English fare, featuring roasts, grills, fresh fish and game in season. The restaurant, which seats 50, gives a wide selection on the à la carte, with starters to appeal to all tastes – over nine to choose from – and main course selections give some unusual and imaginative dishes as well as steaks, mixed grills, crown lamb chops, game pie and grilled lemon sole. There are 11 desserts to conclude, as well as a cheeseboard, coffee and liqueurs.

Centre of Lenham

Lunch
Dinner

Open every day

À la carte £15
Luncheon £11 – £12
Sunday lunch £6.75
Snacks and bar meals from £1.25 – £3.50
House wine from £6 per bottle

Conference facilities

25 bedrooms

AA and RAC recommended

Access, Visa, Amex

THE DOG & BEAR HOTEL

THE SQUARE, LENHAM, MAIDSTONE. (0622) 858219

THROWLEY HOUSE HOTEL

Ashford Road, Sheldwich, Faversham.
Tel: (0795) 539168; Fax: (0795) 535086

Throwley House is a fine Georgian house set in 16 acres of Kent countryside, just two miles south of Faversham and nine miles from Canterbury. The dining room enjoys an enviable reputation for fine cuisine in an intimate and yet unstuffy atmosphere. The views over the gardens tempt many guests to dine *al fresco* in the summer months, perhaps enjoying a game of croquet after Sunday lunch.

Many come to Throwley House to entertain clients or friends, and the private dining room is a much sought-after facility popular with many local business men and women.

One of the hallmarks of Throwley House is its staff, people who take pleasure in pleasing you. Experience is blended with enthusiasm in a team which will help you enjoy the hotel whether you are eating or staying.

The cuisine here does not follow any outside style, but pursues its own innovative approach with an emphasis on local produce.

The starters could offer you Kent game terrine studded with truffle accompanied by an orange and onion compote, home-made noodles baked with a selection of wild mushrooms enhanced by a sherry cream sauce, hot beetroot consommé served with poached quail egg, smoked ham and fresh chervil, or monkfish collops layered between crisp filo pastry swimming on a dill-infused butter.

The main courses are equally imaginative and individual. Pheasant breast encased in a light pastry crust, accompanied by a confit of pheasant and a Madeira wine gravy, Whitstable seafood medley lightly poached in a fresh tomato and fish flavoured essence with basil, pan-fried calf's liver coated with shallots and fresh tarragon, flavoured by balsamic vinegar, or the fish 'catch of the day' could be amongst the dishes you can choose from. All main courses can be cooked in a different way if you wish.

The separate puddings menu could feature three tastes of Kent apples (cinammon crêpe filled with a warm apple compote served with apple brandy ice-cream and cider sorbet) or Kent honey ice-cream.

The wine list features over 100 wines, with a good selection of half bottles, and dessert wines are served by the glass.

The hotel is recommended by the Egon Ronay, Johansens and Ashley Courteney guides, and has AA Rosettes.

On the A251 between Faversham and Ashford, 1 1/2 miles from junction 6 of the M2

Morning coffee 7am–12 noon
Lunch 12noon – 2pm
Afternoon tea 2.30–5pm (pre-booked)
Dinner 7–9.30pm

Closed to non-residents Saturday lunchtime and Sunday evening

À la carte £24.95 set price
Sunday and weekday lunch £16.50 adults; £8.50 children
House wine £9.95 per bottle

Regular vegetarian dishes

Guests are requested not to smoke in the restaurant
Accommodation available
Free car parking
Conference facilities
Croquet lawn with an adjacent health suite, offering a heated indoor swimming pool, spa bath, sauna, sunbeds
Access, Visa, Amex, Diner's Club

Centre of Whitstable

Lunch
Dinner

Closed Monday

À la carte from £20
Lunch £10
House wine £7 per bottle

Vegetarian dishes

Access, Visa

GIOVANNI'S

49 – 55 Canterbury Road, Whitstable.
Tel: (0227) 273034

This lovely restaurant celebrated its 21st anniversary in June 1989. Twenty-one years of quiet success as Whitstable's favourite restaurant, it is esteemed and highly regarded throughout the length and breadth of the county. This has been achieved through the care and devotion of the Ferrari family, whose attention to detail extends throughout the restaurant. This includes the selection of the very best Scottish wild salmon, Aberdeen Angus beef, Kentish lamb and the best game and seafood available. Starters include real turtle soup with sherry, cream of asparagus, minestrone and chicken broth with egg parsley and parmesan cheese. Crabs, lobsters, fresh fish and English roasts are also featured, as well as a mouth-watering selection of Italian classical and regional specialities. The desserts are also exceptional, as is the unobtrusive and attentive service.

Italian and French Cuisine. Whitstable, Kent. Tel: (0227) 273034

MARCHESI

Albion Street, Broadstairs.
Tel: (0843) 62481

Recognition by all the major food guides has done nothing to spoil this superb restaurant. Marchesi was there long before Egon Ronay was born, and is probably the reason that food guides started being published – to select restaurants of true excellence from the many that give poor value for money. The restaurant has been in the hands of one family for over 105 years and its owners, the Roger family, also own and run Broadstairs' famed Royal Albion Hotel. Quality is apparent from the moment you enter and enjoy the delightful decor, the warmth of welcome and the impressive choice of wines on display in the wine racks. The menus give a good choice and, since everything is fresh each day (apart from the well hung meat and properly seasoned game), you are certain of the very best. The fishermen bring their catch here each day, as they have done for generations. Booking is essential, and for their 'French nights' you will need to book weeks in advance.

Centre of Broadstairs

Lunch
Dinner

Open every day

À la carte £15 – £20
Table d'hôte lunch £10.50
House wine £7 per bottle

Theme evenings – French nights

Access, Visa, Amex, Diner's Club

THE MARINA RESORT HOTEL

Harbour Parade, Ramsgate.
Tel: (0843) 588276; Fax: (0843) 586866

Set right on the marina seafront, this fine Resort Hotel offers comfort and service, with good facilities for banqueting, conferences and functions of all types, as well as being an ideal base for exploring the Kent countryside and coastal areas. There are 60 fully *en suite* bedrooms, all of which are equipped with direct dial telephones, remote control colour televisions, hairdryers and trouser presses. The Admiral's Restaurant has earned a first class reputation for fine cuisine, and features the very best of English produce, accented with French flair when appropriate. The carvery menu offers four starters, amongst which the cream of carrot soup with croûtons is highly regarded. These precede a sorbet, which is followed by main courses such as roast leg of pork with apple sauce, liver and sausage casserole, seafood ragoût in white wine sauce and traditional lasagne. There are good desserts too.

Lunch
Afternoon tea
Dinner from 7pm

The restaurant is open in the evening, lunch and afternoon tea are served in Annie's Bar

À la carte £16.50
Table d'hôte £14.50 (includes coffee and mints)
Sunday lunch £10
Bar meals from £1.25 – £5.45
House wine from £7.50 – £20

Conference facilities

60 bedrooms

Access, Visa, Amex, Diner's Club

THE ROYAL OAK

Iden Green, Benenden.
Tel: (0580) 240585

This truly excellent inn has something of a feel of the 'British Raj' about it. Bentwood furniture, punkah fans and filigree wrought iron are something completely different. David and Rita Drewett, owners of The Royal Oak, have won just about every award and accolade imaginable, including 'Best Pub in the South East' (twice), the Dutch Dairy Board's cookery prize (again twice) and many others. There is a superb cold cabinet, along with seafood, salads, poultry, roasts, game, shellfish, crab and lobsters, smoked fish, quiches and cheeses, as well as pulses and at least 25 choices of sweets. Sunday lunch is always popular, so do book in advance, for there is a whole range of dishes on offer from a light snack to a two, three, four or five course meal. The daily specials include dishes such as fresh sole with new potatoes and peas and Bishop's Beef (beef in red wine with Stilton and cream).

Just off the B2086, near Hawkhurst

Lunch
Dinner

À la carte £6 – £12
Sunday lunch £7.50
Snacks from £2
House wine £5.95 per bottle, half bottles available

Vegetarian dishes
Children catered for

Access, Visa, Amex, Diner's Club

Centre of Hawkhurst

Morning coffee
Lunch
Dinner

Closed Sunday night and Monday

À la carte from £18
Sunday lunch £10.50
Bar meals from £4 – £8.50
House wine from £6.95 per bottle

Accommodation available

Access, Visa, Amex, Diner's Club

THE QUEEN'S HEAD HOTEL

Rye Road, Hawkhurst.
Tel: (0580) 753577

The ancient and very lovely Queen's Head Hotel is really a part of the history of this town. An architectural delight, it is as attractive inside as out, with massive oak beams, huge fireplaces, fine accommodation and spacious elegant function facilities, especially for weddings. The hotel has eight double bedrooms and one single, all *en suite* and, under new owners, has been substantially re-appointed to very high standards. Accommodating up to 150 guests, all types of function can be easily catered for. The 30 seater restaurant features both French and English fare and, with dishes like the prawns from the Indian ocean in white wine, glazed with cheese, bacon, soya and garlic, as just one of the imaginative range of starters, followed by local pheasant, roasted in its own marinade, or a fabulous entrecôte Cafe dé Paris in a herb butter, with no less than 15 ingredients, it is small wonder that you need to book.

QUEENS HEAD HOTEL

RYE ROAD, HAWKHURST, KENT. TELEPHONE: 0580 753577

THE MOUNT EDGCUMBE HOUSE HOTEL

The Common, Tunbridge Wells.
Tel: (0892) 26823

The Mount Edgcumbe is acknowledged to be one of the most interesting restaurants in all of Kent. It is several restaurants under one roof, including La Galoche (a cellar grotto) and the elegant main restaurant. Please see page 5 for more information.

THE BARN

Lonsdale Gardens, Tunbridge Wells.
Tel: (0892) 510424

The Barn is the focal point of this lovely town. It is ideally situated for a mid-morning or lunchtime break during shopping, and it is open for lunch and dinner every day. Sample home-made soup, followed by filet de boeuf en croûte. Everything from a light snack to a full meal. Please see page 6 for more information.

SANKEY'S SEAFOOD BAR AND RESTAURANT AT THE GATE

Mount Ephraim, Tunbridge Wells.
Tel: (0892) 511422

There is no better known seafood restaurant in the county. This is Guy Sankey's third restaurant – each more lovely than the last – and each seats over 60 people in auberge-style comfort, in an atmosphere which is both interesting and different. The menus change from day to day, there are different daily specials, and you are always certain to find lobsters, oysters and crabs in abundance. Seafood is bought in fresh and from different suppliers, and there are also one or two meat and vegetarian dishes for those who so prefer. Start with baby scallops grilled with garlic and breadcrumbs, or the Gate's excellent fish soup containing fresh mullet, conger eel and John Dory, served with rouille and gruyère. There are potted shrimps, moules marinière, Dublin Bay prawns (from Scotland), stuffed Corning clams, smoked eel, sweet cured herrings, skate, bass, salmon, Dover sole, crab claws, Greenland prawns, wing of skate and monkfish, not to mention cod, turbot and halibut.

Centre of Tunbridge Wells

Lunch
Dinner

Closed on Sunday

À la carte £6 (inc service)

Vegetarian dishes
Children's helpings on request

Private parties accommodated

Access, Visa

THE SPA HOTEL

Mount Ephraim, Tunbridge Wells.
Tel: (0892) 20331; Telex: 957155 SPATEL; Fax: (0892) 510575

This incomparable hotel was originally built as a mansion for Sir George Kelly, and has been a hotel since 1880. It is often said to be the loveliest hotel in southern England, and the Goring family, who have owned it for many years, are justifiably proud of the fine reputation and high esteem in which The Spa is held.

General Manager Peter Lowe has introduced entirely new menus, giving greater freedom of creativity to his excellent team of chefs who work with the skill and guidance of master chef James Donaldson, the one person who has done so much over the many years to contribute to the hotel's fine name.

The luncheon menu features starters such as iced seasonal melon, six Loch Fyne oysters, cottage cheese with seasonal fruits or parma ham with kiwi fruit.

Main courses offer escalope of pork Holstein, curried lamb with saffron fruit pilaff, Kent sausage with three mustards, brochette of mixed meats, deep-fried goujons of chicken with Cumberland sauce and fillet steak. Profiteroles could conclude.

The table d'hôte dinner menus have a wider range of selections to tempt the palate, with lamb cutlets Reform competing for your attention with

tournedos Café de Paris, picattas of pork Romana and other original and delicious dishes. There is seasonal game of course, and excellent fresh fish creations, enough to satisfy the most exacting requirements. The à la carte is, as you would expect, exceptional. Rainbow trout, Dover sole and fillet steaks are included as main courses, with prices ranging from £11 up to £30 for a chateaubriand with Béarnaise sauce (for two) or roast end of lamb with herbs (again for two) at £26. There are vegetarian dishes, delicious starters and desserts, all rounded off by coffee and petits fours.

The hotel has fine amenities including a beauty therapy clinic, games room, heated indoor swimming pool, fully equipped gym, a dance studio with daily aerobic classes, floodlit tennis courts, sauna, croquet lawn and an adjacent nine hole golf course.

Centre of Tunbridge Wells

Morning coffee
Lunch
Afternoon tea
Dinner

À la carte from £22
Table d'hôte lunch £15
Dinner £19 +
10% service charge

Vegetarian dishes
Leisure facilities
Accommodation available
Conferences and functions catered for

Access, Visa, Amex, Diner's Club

Centre of Tunbridge Wells

Lunch
Dinner
Bar meals

No bar meals Sunday lunchtime
Restaurant closed Sunday dinner
À la carte £22 – £30
Monday to Saturday lunch £13
Dinner Monday to Thursday £15
House wine £7.50 and £9.75 per bottle
Vegetarian dishes

23 rooms ***en suite***
Conferences and private parties accommodated
Weddings catered for

Access, Visa, Amex, Diner's Club

THE ROYAL WELLS INN

Mount Ephraim, Tunbridge Wells.
Tel: (0892) 511188, Fax: (0892) 511908

Overlooking the common from its fine position at the top of Mount Ephraim, The Royal Wells Inn is a most impressive and graceful building, with the royal crest mounted upon its roof. The crest honours Queen Victoria who, as a young princess early in the 19th century, made frequent visits to the hotel. Today it is a traditional, family-run hotel. The original conservatory restaurant makes an elegant backdrop for the cuisine of Head Chef Robert Sloan. The menus change constantly, with unusual dishes alongside the more traditional English roasts, casseroles and steaks. Eels in armagnac and red wine feature, as do Jerusalem artichokes with a Spanish timbale. Other typical dishes include breast of pheasant in port and goujons of monkfish. For dessert, try the ever popular chocolate roulade. There is an extensive wine list to complement the cuisine. For a lighter snack, try Wells Brasserie with its pine furnishings and most interesting motoring memorabilia.

THE SWAN HOTEL

Pantiles, Tunbridge Wells.
Tel: (0892) 541450/27590; Fax: (0892) 541465

It is a great joy to see this ancient hotel reopened after a complete refurbishment. Situated on the historic Pantiles, The Swan has 17 bedrooms, all *en suite*, with direct dial telephones and remote control television. Two of these rooms have four poster beds, and there is a luxury suite with a sitting room, double bedroom and bathroom. Every facility is available for conferences and seminars, and there is also a completely self-contained suite in addition to the general facilities. The Kendal Restaurant seats 40 in spacious luxury, and the menus rival the best the county has to offer. The hotel has a resident pianist on Friday and Saturday evenings. The menus change regularly, and offer a great variety of seasonal English produce, including game, meat, poultry and fresh fish.

Centre of Tunbridge Wells

Morning coffee
Lunch
Afternoon tea
Dinner

Open every day

À la carte £15 – £20
Bar meals from £2
House wine from £8

Conference facilities

Access, Visa

THE SWAN HOTEL

The Pantiles
Royal Tunbridge Wells
Kent

Telephone:
(0892) 541450/27590
Fax: (0892) 541465

THE BROKERS ARMS

5-11 Langton Road, Tunbridge Wells.
Tel: (0892) 541000

Centre of Tunbridge Wells, opposite the famed Spa Hotel

Morning coffee
Lunch
Dinner
Bar meals

Restaurant closed Saturday lunchtime and Sunday evening, limited choice of bar meals Sunday evening

Fixed price dinner £16.95
Lunch £12
Sunday lunch £9.95
Bar meals £3.75
House wine £7.50 per bottle

Real ales

Access, Visa, Amex, Diner's Club, Luncheon Vouchers

Here, in this delightful 15th century free house inn and restaurant, you will find traditional English food and real ales. Greene King Abbot from Suffolk, Harvey's Best (Sussex), Marston's Pedigree from Burton-on-Trent, plus one or more guest ales give a well-chosen variety to choose from. Food, all prepared in the kitchens of the inn's restaurant, places firm emphasis on fresh, locally produced fare, and some five daily specials are featured on the blackboard in addition to the regular menu, so that you have a good choice ranging from fresh fish, steaks and steak sandwiches to garlic mushrooms, chef's paté, moules marinière, ploughman's lunches and others too numerous to detail. Peter and Myra Chipchase are your hosts, and The Broker's Arms is one of the only two free houses in Tunbridge Wells. The restaurant seats 35 and there is a fine functions room where parties and weddings can be catered for up to 40 people.

Famished in Felixstowe?

Hungry in Holyhead?

Peckish in Perth?

Ravenous in Roscommon?

WHERE TO EAT

The discerning diner's guide to restaurants throughout Britain and Ireland

Copies available from bookshops or direct from the publishers
Kingsclere Publications Ltd
Use the Order Form On Page 51

THE SPOTTED DOG

Smarts Hill, Penhurst.
Tel: (0892) 870253/870949

The Spotted Dog is well-known for its magnificent views across the Medway Valley, and it attracts visitors from near and far. The 15th century building started life as a row of cottages, and it was established as an inn in 1520. There is a wealth of beams throughout, and four fireplaces including an inglenook to keep out winter chills, creating a special atmosphere of warmth and old world charm. The bar offers a wide choice of real ales, and the home-cooked, traditional English and Continental food includes steak and kidney pie, spotted dick and lasagne. The restaurant menu features French-based cuisine, with traditional lunches on Sundays. Vegetarian dishes are available in the bar and the restaurant. The inn is a free house and is cheerfully managed by Andy and Nikki Tucker.

On Smarts Hill, off the B2176 above the village of Penshurst

Coffee from 11am
Lunch 12 noon – 2.15pm
Dinner 7 – 9.30pm
Bar meals 12 noon – 2.15pm; 7 – 9.30pm

Restaurant closed Monday, Tuesday and Sunday evening

À la carte £15
Sunday lunch £12.75
Bar meals from £1.85 – £4.45
House mine £7.45 per bottle; £1.40 per glass

Vegetarian dishes
Real ales

Access, Visa

THE ROSE AND CROWN

High Street, Tonbridge.
Tel: (0732) 357966

This 18th century establishment is a Trusthouse Forte hotel, complete with all the amenities one associates with the group. The Chaucer Restaurant offers good value for money, with a selection of eight starters and many unusual speciality main courses. Please see page 7 for more information.

THE KING'S HEAD RESTAURANT

Bessels Green, Sevenoaks.
Tel: (0732) 452081 – inn/740279 – restaurant

The country atmosphere of the traditional inn-on-the-green is evident in every aspect of the fine fare provided. The food includes the whole range from a light snack at the bar, with real ales or wine by the glass, to a first class restaurant menu with over a dozen starters, and as many main course selections. French onion soup, vichyssoise (hot or cold), Greek fish salad, seafood au gratin and gravadlax are just a few examples from the range of first courses. Main courses include poached Scottish salmon salad, gigot of lamb with mint butter, pork fillets layered with cream and cheese, fillet or rump steaks, veal cutlets Sevilliana, plus steak and venison pie are amongst the main course selections. Sample fresh fruit flan, baked honey, almond and apple pudding with cream, and linzertorte (raspberries with almond pastry and cream, from the desserts. All the dishes are home-made and the menu changes every eight weeks.

Near Sevenoaks

Morning coffee
Lunch
Dinner

Restaurant closed Saturday lunchtime
Bar meals every lunchtime except Sunday

À la carte £12.50
Sunday lunch £6
House wine £5.30 per bottle; 95p per glass

Centre of Brasted

Lunch
Dinner

Open every day

Table d'hôte £5 – £9.50
Snacks and bar meals from £1.50
Wines from £4.95 – a fine selection

Garden for ***al fresco*** *dining*

THE WHITE HART

High Street, Brasted, Westerham.
Tel: (0959) 62814

The White Hart is part of the very history of Kent. It has featured in novels and biographies, as well as just about everything ever written about the Battle of Britain. It was the inn where the Spitfire and Hurricane pilots came after each battle to drink to fallen comrades, and prepared for the next encounter. Food was rationed in those days, but now The White Hart is a place of peace and plenty. The winter months offer delicious roasts, stews, casseroles and pies, whilst the summer fare includes salads and fish dishes, followed by fresh fruit and cream. The garden draws enthusiasts too, with displays of petunias in June, July and August. There is limited accommodation, and this is a good base from which to explore Winston Churchill's house at Chartwell, General Wolfe's family home, Quebec House, as well as great houses such as Penshurst Place and Hever Castle.

THE KING'S ARMS

Meopham Green, Meopham.
Tel: (0474) 813042; Fax: (0474) 812497

If you wanted to show a visitor from overseas what a truly English village inn should be like, then the King's Arms at Meopham Green would be the perfect role model. Mullioned windows look out onto the village green where, during the summer months, cricket is usually in progress. Inside, flickering firelight from open log fires casts shadows across oak beams, and reflects from horse brasses and sparkling glasses. The 50 seat restaurant, with soft delightful decor, is further enhanced by a permanent extension into a marquee and garden. The marquee itself seats 60, and this is an ideal venue for weddings and private parties, as well as business meetings and conferences. The food is highly regarded, as it offers great variety and a reasonable pricing policy. Steaks and fresh fish always feature on the menu. The chef's specials include beef Stilton, tournedos Rossini, duck à l'orange, chicken Kiev and steak au poivre.

Centre of Meopham

Morning coffee
Lunch
Dinner

Open every day

À la carte £14.50
Sunday lunch £7.30 (three courses)
Bar snacks from £1 – £6
House wine from £1.50

Conference facilities

Access, Mastercard, Amex

THE HENGIST

7/9 High Street, Aylesford, Maidstone.
Tel: (0622) 719273; Fax: (0622) 715027

This restaurant is named after the first Saxon king of Kent and offers imaginative names to complement the imaginative cuisine. Here, starters are the 'Initial Skirmish' and main courses the 'Main Battle'. Smoked goose breast with Oxford sauce and roast duck with spicy orange are amongst the dishes. Please see page 8 for more information.

Near Maidstone

Lunch
Dinner

Open Tuesday to Saturday, except Saturday lunchtime

Set dinner £25
Set lunch £17.30

Vegetarian dishes
Children catered for

Private parties accommodated

Access for disabled guests

Access, Visa, Amex, Diner's Club, Carte Blanche

SUEFFLÉ

The Green, Bearsted, Maidstone.
Tel: (0622) 37065

This restaurant began life as two cottages, in an ideal setting beside the village green. Owner Sue Dunderdale (hence the name of the restaurant) has created an intimate, bistro-style restaurant within this traditional setting. There is a patio for open air dining in summer, and overall the restaurant can seat 44. There is no formal menu, as dishes are taken from the blackboard. A possible meal could include moules marinière, followed by rack of lamb with Madeira sauce, and strawberry timbale to finish. The dishes are a mixture of classic cuisine with an individual finish from chef Andy Blyth. The wine list includes a reasonably priced selection of French regional bottles. There is car parking on site.

Whilst we believe that all factual details are correct, we suggest that readers check, when making reservations, that prices and other facts quoted meet their requirements.

Kentish battlements at Dover

THE SHANT HOTEL AND PRINCE OF WALES

East Sutton, Near Maidstone.
Tel: (0622) 842235

'Where to Eat in Kent' is proud to be able to feature again The Shant Hotel and Prince of Wales. Here, standards are not just maintained – and they have never been less than excellent – they are improved each year, to add new dimensions to the facilities, ideas and comforts. A new restaurant has opened in the last 12 months, with a quality of food and service comparable with the top establishments in the county. The hotel has facilities for every type of function, and is particularly suitable for private parties, business lunches and dinners, seminars, conferences and directors' dining. The Prince of Wales, which is an inn within the hotel, caters for light lunches and dinners, offering everything from a simple ploughman's lunch or sandwich to curries, pastas, casseroles and daily specials. Eleven bedrooms, all *en suite*, have every comfort such as colour TV and tea/coffee making facilities.

Near Maidstone

Lunch
Dinner

Meals from £3.95
House wine £5.50 per bottle

Conference and function facilities

Accommodation available

Access, Visa, Amex

Full details on page 59

Please telephone for directions

Morning coffee
Lunch
Dinner

Open every day

À la carte from £8.50
Bar meals from £2
House wine from £5.65 per bottle

Vegetarian dishes

THE SHIP INN AND SMUGGLER'S RESTAURANT

Teynham, near Sittingbourne.
Tel: (0795) 521404

George East, editor of Food & Drink Magazine, wrote thus of The Ship Inn & Smuggler's Restaurant, when he visited it in June 1988. 'In truth, I have had but a handful of memorable visits to table in twenty years of following the dubious profession of eating for a living. On the day of my visit to The Ship, I had one of the most memorable meals of my life.' There is much more to The Ship than just the superb food. Over 175 single malt whiskies are stocked, and the international wine list recently led to The Ship being voted Wine Pub of the Year by Grants of St James. The landlord, Alec Heard, is a character indeed. Bearded, jovial and extrovert, he appears on the pages of the menu in varied garb – as a pirate, a Nazi officer and others. To try and describe the variety and quality of the food would need a whole chapter. Everything is home-made, including fondues with crispy French bread, seafood (lobster in particular), shellfish and Kent lamb – everything for every taste.

THE SHIP INN & SMUGGLERS RESTAURANT IS WELL OFF THE BEATEN TRACK, YOU WILL NEED TO TELEPHONE FOR DIRECTIONS. (0795) 521404.

THE DOG AND BEAR HOTEL

The Square, Lenham, near Maidstone.
Tel: (0622) 858219

This delightful old coaching inn dates from 1602, and the royal coat of arms displayed above the main entrance reflects the visit of Queen Anne to this establishment in 1704. The food is traditional English in approach, with steak, crown lamb chops and game pie amongst other dishes. For more information, please see page 9.

THROWLEY HOUSE HOTEL

Ashford Road, Sheldwich, Faversham.
Tel: (0795) 539168; Fax: (0795) 535086

This fine Georgian house is set in 16 acres of Kent countryside. The cuisine does not conform to any style except Throwley House's own, and is all the better for this. Sample Kent game terrine, then Whitstable seafood medley, with Kent honey ice-cream for dessert. Please see page 11 for more information.

GIOVANNI'S

49–55 Canterbury Road, Whitstable.
Tel: (0227) 273034

This lovely restaurant is over 20 years old, and it is highly regarded throughout Kent. Its success is due in no small way to the dedication of the Ferrari family, whose attention to detail is evident throughout. Sample Aberdeen Angus beef, or Kent lamb amongst the main courses. Real turtle soup to start with. Please see page 12 for more information.

Thanks to the vital support of advertisers and readers alike, more comprehensive guides are being prepared. Each guide is freshly researched, revised and updated each year.

On the A28 Margate to Canterbury road

Morning coffee
Lunch
Dinner

Open every day

À la carte from £7.50 to 12
Bar meals from £1 to £6.50
House wine from £5 – £12

Garden

Barbecues in summer

THE ROYAL OAK

60 Island Road, Upstreet, near Canterbury.
Tel: (0227) 86314

'Why on earth didn't we discover this place before?' is the question you are likely to ask yourself after you find The Royal Oak at Upstreet. There is no simple answer except perhaps that Upstreet is a village you might tend to drive through in a hurry to be somewhere else. Next time – stop here. This fine inn includes accommodation with *en suite* bedrooms, colour televisions and tea/coffee making facilities. Bar meals offer club sandwiches, home-made soup, toasted sandwiches, chilli con carne, steaks, jumbo sausages with baked potatoes and cheese and salad amongst others. The restaurant proper gives excellent value and has favourites such as steak Diane, steak au poivre, tournedos Rossini, half roast chicken, gammon and pineapple, trout Bretonne and a daily chef's special.

THE ROYAL ALBION HOTEL

Albion Street, Broadstairs.
Tel: (0800) 521130; Telex: (0843) 965761

Broadstairs' famed Royal Albion Hotel is part of the history of this lovely and historic town. It was here that Charles Dickens wrote much of *Nicholas Nickleby*, and the hotel owns the original letter that Dickens wrote to a close friend, praising both Broadstairs and the hotel. There is always a lot going on at the Royal Albion – golfing weekends, trips to France and special gourmet evenings. Hotel director Peter Roger is a wine expert, a Chevalier of the Order of St Vincent de Flandres, and throughout the year he arranges special wine events. The hotel is an ideal venue for business lunches and conferences, with a 100 seater function room, a private boardroom and secretarial services available. Special banqueting menus can be arranged for all types of function. The views over Broadstairs' harbour from the hotel are breathtaking. The Roger family also own Marchesis (see a separate entry in the guide) and guests are free to dine here or in the hotel.

Centre of Broadstairs

Lunch
Dinner

À la carte from £15.50
House wine from £5.75 per bottle

Conference and banqueting facilities

20 rooms accommodation

Gourmet evenings and wine tasting events

Access, Visa, Amex, Diner's Club

THE ROYAL ALBION HOTEL, ALBION ST. TEL: FREE ON 0800 521130

Centre of Broadstairs

Lunch
Dinner

Open every day (last orders 9.30pm in Winter, 10pm in Summer)

À la carte from £5 upwards
Table d'hôte lunch £5.95
House wine from £5

Vegetarian dishes

Access, Visa, Amex

THE MAD CHEF'S BISTRO

35 Harbour Street, Broadstairs.
Tel: (0843) 69304/604609

This characterful, cosmopolitan bistro brings delight to everyone who has the pleasure of finding it. Overlooking the harbour at Broadstairs, the atmosphere is both seafaring and piratical, and this is no gimmick as the owner, the 'Mad Chef' himself, is a seafarer who has come in from the cold and takes great pride in this fine restaurant. The bistro is recognised by the major food guide, and specialises in seafood, especially lobsters, crabs, local fish and shellfish. There are 17 vegetarian and wholefood dishes, as well as steaks, and choosing your main course is by no means an easy decision. There are 14 starters to choose from on the main menu – all seafood dishes, including clams, prawns oysters, mussels and soft roes. All the dishes are reasonably priced.

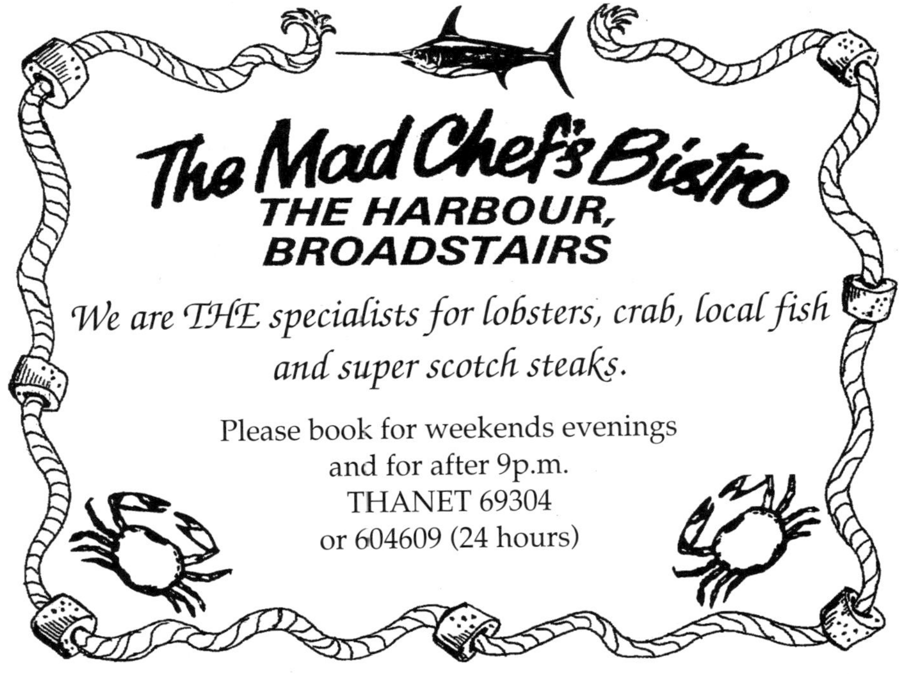

MARCHESI

Albion Street, Broadstairs.
Tel: (0843) 62481

Highly thought of by all the major food guides, this restaurant has been around much longer than any of the publications that sing its praises. Owned by the Roger family, the warmth of welcome afforded all guests brings people flocking back to sample the well hung meat and game, as well as the fresh fish and seafood. Please see page 13 for more information.

THE MARINA RESORT HOTEL

Harbour Parade, Ramsgate.
Tel: (0843) 588276; Fax: (0843) 586866

Set right on the marina sea front, this fine Resort Hotel offers comfort and service, and is a good base from which to explore the Kent countryside. The Admiral's Restaurant serves a carvery menu, with starters including cream of carrot soup, and good desserts. Please see page 14 for more information.

WALLETT'S COURT

West Cliffe, St Margaret's at Cliffe, Dover.
Tel: (0304) 852424

Wallett's Court is a traditional, reasonably priced hotel which combines facets of middle ages architecture from Middle Ages right through to 17th century style. The cuisine has an appropriately country-feel and simplicity for this area of Kent. An inexpensive set price menu is the order of the day during the week, with the addition of a five course gourmet meal on Saturdays. A possible meal could begin with huntsman's platter (smoked duck, pork terrine and bacon in a Cumberland sauce) followed by turbot with crab and mustard sauce. Try raspberry syllabub for dessert. The accommodation here (7 rooms all *en suite*) is comfortable and reasonably priced. Chris and Lea Oakley are your hosts, with Chris doing all the cooking.

On the B2058

Dinner

Open Tuesday to Saturday

Set dinner £16 – £23
House wine £7

Vegetarian dishes
Children's helpings

7 rooms accommodation

Private parties catered for

Access, Visa

Take the A258 Deal to Sandwich road, Finglesham is half way between.

Morning coffee
Lunch
Dinner

Open every day

À la carte £10
Bar meals £2.25 – £3.95
House wine from £5.50 per bottle

THE CROWN INN AT FINGLESHAM

The Street, Finglesham, Deal.
Tel: (0304) 612555

'Where to Eat in Kent' discovered this most delightful country inn as a direct result of repeated recommendations from readers of the guide There is no better accolade, and it is good to see such a successful inn set in an off-the-beaten-track location. Here there are real ales, good sound home-cooking and a fine atmosphere, set within a building of old flagstones and inglenook open log fires. There is a daily special on the blackboard – several in fact – with steak and kidney pie, paprika beef, fillet of cod creole style, Cinzano kidney and others. Three course Sunday lunch is just £6.25 and table d'hôte dinner £6.95 on Friday nights only. The à la carte has plenty to choose from with starters of whitebait, pâté and toast, prawn cocktail and mussels in garlic. The main courses include a delectable breast of chicken Napoleon, fillet of sole Walewska, pork fillets in Calvados, Burgundy lamb cutlets and mixed grill. The desserts include crème caramel, and apples and blackberries with cream.

THE CROWN INN *The Street, Finglesham, Deal. Tel: (0304) 612555*

THE WIFE OF BATH

4 Upper Bridge Street, Wye.
Tel: (0233) 812540

Using the experience gained by working at Ransomes of London, the new owner of the Wife of Bath is building a reputation for being the host of a fine restaurant. The special business lunches available on the French-influenced menu show that the management is serious about catering for a cross-section of the public. Customers can choose from starters like soup of the day, or a tartlet of spinach and mushroom purée with quails, eggs glazed with hollandaise. These could be followed, perhaps, by suprême of chicken stuffed with tropical fruit and poached in a coconut cream sauce or maybe a roast rack of English lamb with a herb crust and a fresh rosemary gravy. Such luxurious sounding main courses are complemented by a selection of home-made ice-creams, sorbets and puddings, and a range of wines with over 50 labels to choose from. It is a menu that the Wife of Bath herself would surely approve of.

Off the A28, near Ashford

Lunch
Dinner

Closed Sunday night and Monday lunchtime

À la carte £13.95
Evening meal £18.95
Sunday lunch £12.95
House wine £7.75 per bottle

Visa, Mastercard

EASTWELL MANOR

Eastwell Park, Boughton Aluph, near Ashford.
Tel: (0233) 635751

Eastwell Manor is well-known as a quality establishment offering superior standards of hospitality and accommodation. The beautiful wood-panelled restaurant is renowned for its superb food, excellent service and is the current holder of the coveted Country Restaurant of the Year (*Good Food Guide*).

The hotel's food is exceptional and combines gourmet French dishes with some traditional English cooking. Mark Clayton, the Head Chef, has brought a new dimension to Eastwell's food. He uses the finest ingredients, many of them local, and concentrates on flavours rather than current trends and appearances.

Dishes to start with, such as fresh ravioli filled with spinach and Caprini goats cheese in a fennel butter sauce, and the light scallop mousse on a bed of carrots in a langoustine and dill sauce, are fairly typical of the chef's style. Main courses such as sea bass and bream on a bed of spinach in a mussel and ginger sauce, and braised knuckle of veal with lentils in a Madeira sauce, combine the light modern touch of the fish to the more robust classical combination of the knuckle of veal.

To finish the experience, a Jamaican flan with bananas as its main ingredient, or maybe some fine English cheeses served with fresh warm walnut bread. The menu changes daily to accommodate seasonal fare but the concept and standards remain the same.

Portions are generous and the chef is very happy to talk to individual customers regarding any personal requirements.

Eastwell's cellar is very well stocked with wines from all over the world, including California and New Zealand. The range includes a selection of good house wines and extends to the world renowned Château Pétrus. A large selection of half bottles are also available.

	À la carte from £27	
Near Ashford	*Dinner £24*	
	Set lunch £12.75 – £16.50	*Accommodation available*
Lunch	*Sunday lunch £17.50*	
	Traditional afternoon tea £8	
Dinner	*Kentish cream tea from £4.50*	*Access, Visa*
	House wine from £14	

Off the B2077

Morning coffee
Lunch
Dinner

From £1.50 – £10
Sunday lunch £6.50 (three courses)
House wine from £5.70

Real ales – Harvey's, Adnam's, Tetleys and Bombardier

Vegetarian dishes

No credit cards

THE QUEEN'S ARMS

Egerton Forstal, Ashford.
Tel: (0233) 76386

In the very heart of rural Kent, you will find this delightful family-run free house. Off the beaten track, the Queen's Arms is a perfect example of how an English country inn should look – and be run. Valerie Hogben takes enormous pride in the superb home-cooking, and her enthusiasm is reflected in every aspect of this, sparkling inn. Only fresh prawns are used in the prawn cocktail, all the soup is home-made and the season's fresh produce is always used. The Sunday roast is served with six fresh vegetables, and horseradish from the field instead of a jar. There are four real ales, including Bombardier. This is particularly appropriate as that legend of boxing, Bombardier Billy Wells, was Valerie's father. Try the home-made chicken, ham and leek pie, or a lovely tuna quiche (made without eggs). There is a daily special on the blackboard, but the *pièce de resistance* is the roast beef, always an H-bone or topside, with Yorkshire pudding.

THE QUEENS ARMS
Egerton Forstal, Ashford. Tel: (0233) 76386

FLEUR DE LIS

Brenzett, Romney Marsh.
Tel: (06794) 234

A most attractive inn, located between Appledore and New Romney, in the village of Brenzett. The Fleur de Lis has been completely refurbished, and owners Pat and Reg Harding have wasted no time turning the inn into one of the busiest and friendliest hostelries in the Marsh. The restaurant menu offers a changing variety of fare, and you will find starters such as prawn cocktail and real home-made soup, followed by scampi, steaks, cod and chips, home-made shepherd's pie, haddock and Dover sole. A good selection of desserts follow. The inn has nine double bedrooms, all centrally heated, and sporting colour televisions. The rooms are good value at £15 per person, per night. There is a garden, with tables, swings and chairs, for the children. Good bar snacks are always available.

Centre of Brenzett

Lunch 11am – 2pm
Dinner 7 – 11pm
Supper licence

À la carte £8 – £12
Sunday lunch £6
Bar meals from £1
House wine from £4.80

Garden

Eight rooms accommodation

On the A28 near Tenterden

Lunch
Dinner

Closed Sunday evening and all day Monday

À la carte £14
Lunch £10
House wine £6 per bottle

Private parties by arrangement

Access, Visa

GARDNER'S RESTAURANT

57 High Street, Rolvenden.
Tel: (0580) 241992

Set in England's very own 'garden county', Adrian Gardner's cottage restaurant aims to cultivate a sociable, yet relatively inexpensive, atmosphere in which to dine. Customers who decide to patronise the restaurant (a garden terrace is also available) can enjoy a candlelit ambience in which to choose their meal. The combined styles of England and France produce main courses such as magret breast of duck with sherry and lime sauce, and all dishes are accompanied by fresh local vegetables, acquired daily from Covent Garden. Complementary to the menu, which is changed every six weeks, are wines that can be chosen from a list containing over 60 labels from countries like England and France, as well as Australia, Chile, the United States and the Lebanon. In addition to providing the above, Gardner's Restaurant is also available for Sunday lunches, as well as private parties by special arrangement.

Gardner's Restaurant, 57 High Street, Rolvenden, Kent TN17 4LP
Telephone 0580 241992

THE EIGHT BELLS

High Street, Tenterden.
Tel: (058 06) 2788

0580 762788

An ancient inn right in the centre of the graceful town of Tenterden, The Eight Bells is always lively. It is very English with its dark oak beams and timbers, yet the concept is very much in the French style, taking advantage of the new licensing laws to cater to the needs of tourist and visitor alike, throughout the day. The restaurant is really a bistro, with a constantly changing menu and specials of the day (five or six to choose from). Everything is home-cooked with an accent on fresh local produce, and the kitchen has gained a wide local following. There are excellent facilities for private celebrations and other functions, with a large and beautifully designed function room (complete with private bar and dance floor) which can cater for up to 100 guests. The dining room seats 46. It is advisable to book in advance at weekends.

Centre of Tenterden

Morning coffee
Lunch
Dinner

À la carte £10
Lunch £6.95
Snacks from £1.50
House wine £5.60 per bottle

Access, Visa

On the A28

Lunch
Dinner

Closed Sunday and Monday

À la carte £15
Lunch £9.50
House wine from £16 per bottle

Vegetarian dishes

Access, Visa, Amex

YE MADES RESTAURANT

High Street, Biddenden.
Tel: (0580) 291306

Residing in the old village of Biddenden, Ye Mades Restaurant is housed in an ancient cottage building that once played host to Flemish weavers. Since their long distant departure, the restaurant's present owner has strived to manage the establishment in a manner where only the best will do, and whilst settled amongst the polished oak furniture and blazing open fires one can sample the fruits of that philosophy. Duck with wild strawberries, garlic and pine kernel tartlet and a seafood pancake chevion can all be found on the menu. The dishes change monthly to accommodate the fresh fish and game that seasonally become available. Starters like curried mushrooms, herbal mousse and Stilton and grape pastries precede the main courses. The cuisine overall is a blend of English and French cooking styles, combining new recipes with old favourites.

THE BELL

Smarden.
Tel: (023 377) 283

As soon as you enter The Bell, you know this is the real thing. The floor is made of huge ancient flagstones; the massive oak beams, great logs in cavernous inglenook fireplaces and genuine antique furniture will make you feel that you have stepped backward in time. Small wonder that this inn was chosen to be featured in the American magazine *Newsweek*. Spacious gardens with flowering shrubs, trees and flower borders, set in the very heart of the garden of England, with tables and benches to enjoy your meal and drinks *al fresco* if you wish. The good home-cooked food ranges from simple sandwiches and ploughman's lunches to home-baked ham and gammon steaks, Cumberland pie, fillet and rump steaks, chilli con carne, steak and kidney pie and lasagne, to name but a few from a wide selection. Crunch cake, bread pudding and apple crumble are some of the desserts featured. Booking in advance recommended (not Saturday nights).

Smarden

Lunch
Dinner

À la carte from £1.10 – £8.25
House wine £4.95 per bottle; £1.10 per glass

Children catered for

Accommodation

A garden and children's room

No smoking area

Access, Visa

Smarden (023 377) 283

0233 770283

Centre of Headcorn

Lunch
Dinner

À la carte £10
Snacks from £1
House wine £5.35 per bottle

Live entertainment
Barbecues in summer

Accommodation

THE KING'S ARMS

High Street, Headcorn.
Tel: (0622) 890216

'Where to Eat in Kent' is again delighted to feature this fine English country inn, The King's Arms. It is hoped that we have contributed to the great success of this inn, which has led to its having had to almost double the size of the restaurant – by public demand. The reason, of course, is the lovely home-cooked food for which the inn is renowned. Fresh fish every day with fresh dressed crab, shell-on prawns in garlic, salmon steaks, plaice and cod. A house speciality is the grilled fresh sardine dish, and the home-baked gammon is another you should try. At £6.50, the roast Sunday lunches are exceptional value and it is wise to book in advance. The menu varies from day to day, but you are almost always certain of the superb fillet of beef Stroganoff, the fresh plaice with cheese sauce, and the steak and kidney pie. There is live entertainment in the bar almost every week, and the inn has a nice garden with outdoor barbecues in summer.

THE KINGS ARMS
HEADCORN

THE LORD RAGLAN

Chart Hill Road, Staplehurst.
Tel: (0622) 843747

Set deep in the Kentish countryside, miles from anywhere, The Lord Raglan inn is situated in a country lane overlooking meadowland. In this seemingly idyllic location, the inn provides its customers with a plethora of dishes, beginning with starters such as Raglan pâté with toast, leek and Stilton soup or blini (Russian pancakes served with caviar, onion and sour cream). These could be followed by pan-fried Dover sole or fresh trout. Also available are char-grilled rump steak with garlic butter, as well as veal cordon bleu, beef Stroganoff, breast of pigeon with port and cream sauce and chicken Wellington (a chicken breast in puff pastry, served with a mushroom sauce). Vegetarians are catered for, with special dishes prepared on request.

On the A229

Lunch
Dinner

No meals Sunday/Monday evenings

À la carte £12 – £15
Sunday lunch £9.95
Bar meals from £2
House wine from £6.20

Vegetarian dishes

Access, Visa

On the B2079

Dinner
Lunch Sunday only

Open for dinner Tuesday - Saturday

À la carte £15
Sunday lunch £8.50
House wine from £6.70 per bottle

Vegetarian dishes

Access, Visa, Amex, Diner's Club

THE PLACE IN MARDEN RESTAURANT

27 High Street, Marden.
Tel: (0622) 832467

Located in the centre of the hop and orchard growing area of Kent, the village of Marden not only plays host to the famous annual Marden Fruit Show, but also to The Place Restaurant. Seating 60 guests, this cottage restaurant offers an extensive range of dishes (six course gourmet meals available on Fridays), with a strong emphasis placed on fresh fish dishes, using raw materials personally selected by the owner. Bearing this in mind, one can choose starters ranging from Beluga caviar served with iced vodka to mushrooms in a blue cheese sauce, to be followed by main courses such as trout Cleopatra (fresh river trout with capers and prawns), steak Diane or suprême de volaille cardinale (a plump breast of chicken, stuffed with seafood and served in a lobster sauce). Vegetarians are also catered for, with various omelettes and dishes like stir-fried vegetable pancakes to choose from.

ORDER FORM

To:
KINGSCLERE PUBLICATIONS LTD.
Highfield House, 2 Highfield Avenue, Newbury, Berkshire RG14 5DS

Please send me

____copies of ***WHERE TO EAT*** in **BRISTOL, BATH, AVON, SOMERSET & WILTSHIRE** at £2.95 £____
____copies of ***WHERE TO EAT*** in the **CHANNEL ISLANDS** at £1.25 £____
____copies of ***WHERE TO EAT*** in **CORNWALL** at £2.50 £____
____copies of ***WHERE TO EAT*** in **CUMBRIA & THE LAKE DISTRICT** at £1.95 £____
____copies of ***WHERE TO EAT*** in **DORSET & SOUTH WILTSHIRE** at £2.95 £____
____copies of ***WHERE TO EAT*** in **EAST ANGLIA & ESSEX** at £2.50 £____
____copies of ***WHERE TO EAT*** in **EAST MIDLANDS** at £1.95 £____
____copies of ***WHERE TO EAT*** in **GLOUCESTERSHIRE, OXFORDSHIRE & THE COTSWOLDS** at £2.50 £____
____copies of ***WHERE TO EAT*** in **HAMPSHIRE & THE NEW FOREST** at £1.95 £____
____copies of ***WHERE TO EAT*** in **IRELAND** at £3.50 £____
____copies of ***WHERE TO EAT*** in **KENT** at £2.50 £____
____copies of ***WHERE TO EAT*** in **NORTH EAST ENGLAND** at £1.95 £____
____copies of ***WHERE TO EAT*** in **NORTH WEST ENGLAND** at £2.50 £____
____copies of ***WHERE TO EAT*** in **SCOTLAND** at £2.50 £____
____copies of ***WHERE TO EAT*** in **SURREY** at £2.50 £____
____copies of ***WHERE TO EAT*** in **SUSSEX** at £2.50 £____
____copies of ***WHERE TO EAT*** in **THAMES & CHILTERNS** at £2.50 £____
____copies of ***WHERE TO EAT*** in **WALES** at £3.50 £____
____copies of ***WHERE TO EAT*** in **YORKSHIRE & HUMBERSIDE** at £2.50 £____

p&p at £0.50 (single copy), £1 (2-5 copies), £2 (6 copies)

GRAND TOTAL £____

Name . . . .
Address . . . .
. . . .
Postcode . . . . Cheque enclose £. . . . .

Your help in answering the following would be appreciated:

(1) Did you buy this guide at a SHOP ❑ TOURIST OFFICE ❑ GARAGE ❑ OTHER ❑

(2) Are any of your favourite eating places *not* listed in this guide? If so, could you please supply names and locations . . . .
. . . .
. . . .

THE KENNEL HOLT COUNTRY HOUSE HOTEL

Cranbrook.
Tel: (0580) 712032; Fax: (0580) 712931

The Kennel Holt Hotel is now regarded as one of the finest country house hotels in the country, and the reputation for excellence and value for money has contributed to the great popularity which it now enjoys. David and Jane Misseldine have taken the fullest possible advantage of the rural setting of this exquisite country house, and it is here that peace and tranquillity take on a new meaning.

Located on the main road between Goudhurst and Cranbrook, you will have to keep an eye open for the hotel's sign at the roadside, for The Kennel Holt is to be found, set in landscaped gardens, down a private drive, well away from the sounds of traffic. The house itself is Elizabethan, and is both elegant and graceful, yet there is an informality that will put you at your ease the moment you arrive. This is the ideal place at which to stay if you are visiting the area, as you are well located to visit Scotney Castle, Bodiam, Leeds Castle, Headcorn Aerodrome (with its famous parachute club and London Flight Centre training school) – whilst Sissinghurst Castle is within walking distance.

The restaurant seats 32, and on Friday and Saturday evenings there is usually a pianist to create the right atmosphere in which to enjoy the fine food. Guests are welcomed first with drinks (waiter-served crystal) in one of the two fine lounges, before moving on to the dining room. However, because of the way in which the menu changes, literally from day to day, it is most difficult to do more than give an impression of the variety of cuisine available. The great British traditional dishes feature large on all menus, with the famed roast beef of Olde England, Yorkshire pudding and fresh vegetables, properly hung game in season, poultry, fresh fish, seafood and Kentish lamb.

There is a wide choice on the daily luncheon menu, as chefs Ian Best and Peter Miller give every bit as much attention to this as to the dinner menu. You may choose between the three course lunch at £11.50 or a full five course spread at £18.75.

The quality of the wine cellar is well-known, with English wines from Lamberhurst, Penshurst, and Chiddingstone featuring strongly, and a selection of fine Burgundies also prominent. Particular attention is paid to the selection of the house wines.

On the B2189

Lunch
Tea
Dinner

Closed Sunday evenings except for residents

Dinner £19.75
Lunch (3 course) £11.50
Sunday lunch £16.75
House wine £7.45 per bottle

Ten bedrooms, all ***en suite***

Access, Visa, Amex, Diner's Club

On the B2169 near Lamberhurst

Morning coffee
Lunch
Dinner

À la carte from £5
Bar meals from £2
House wine from £5.95

Vegetarian dishes
Children welcome

THE ELEPHANT'S HEAD

Hook Green, Lamberhurst.
Tel: (0892) 890279

The Elephant's Head is situated in the heart of the Kent countryside, overlooking sheep pastures and woodland. Midway between Tunbridge Wells and the village of Lamberhurst, it occupies one of the loveliest settings in the county. At The Elephant's Head you will find a genuine olde worlde inn, over 500 years old, with beamed ceilings and blazing log fires. The modern restaurant seats 28, with an evening menu specialising in top quality local produce. House specials include steaks, roast duckling, salmon steaks, trout, chicken, scampi and lasagne. The chef's special is very popular, and the inn has a good salad bar. The lunch menu features many old favourites, including steak and kidney pie made with real ale. Home-made soups are available both lunchtimes and evenings. A full range of Harveys real ales, vintage ports and reasonably priced wines is complemented by attractive gardens, including a children's play area. There are two large car parks.

THE ROYAL OAK

Iden Green, Benenden.
Tel: (0580) 240585

The Royal Oak has the style of the British Raj, with punkah fans, bentwood furniture and filigree wrought iron. It has won many awards for its cuisine, as there is a superb cold cabinet featuring salads, seafood, poultry and game. Please see page 15 for more information.

THE QUEEN'S HEAD HOTEL

Rye Road, Hawkhurst.
Tel: (0580) 753577

This ancient hotel is as attractive inside as it is out. The 30 seater restaurant features both French and English cuisine, with dishes such as prawns in white wine glazed with cheese, bacon, soya and garlic. It has been substantially refurbished in recent times. Please see page 16 for more information.

Centre of Goudhurst

Morning coffee
Lunch
Tea

Snacks from £1 – £5

WEEKS OF GOUDHURST

High Street, Goudhurst.
Tel: (0580) 211380

Weeks is both a bakery and a café/restaurant. Over the years it has built up a substantial local following for its produce and its success has generated shops throughout the Weald of Kent. There are now branches in Battle, Mayfield, Pembury, Heathfield, Wadhurst, Staplehurst, Tenterden, Cranbrook, Headcorn and Yalding, and in Goudhurst there is a restaurant as well. Weeks is reminiscent of the bakeries of old. Here you can buy real bread, still warm from the oven, along with a whole range of buns, gâteaux, cream cakes, spongy confections and scones. The restaurant is open all day from 9am, serving coffee, snacks, teas and lunches (including Sunday). There are soups and starters, cottage pie, lasagne, moussaka, jacket potatoes with all kinds of fillings, salads, ploughman's lunches and daily specials too. The desserts speak for themselves and the choice is extensive and tempting. Prices are also very reasonable and the staff friendly.

Next to the Lamberhurst vineyards

Lunch
Dinner

No food Monday evening

À la carte £6.50 – £12.50
Sunday lunch (three course) £7.50
House wine from £5.25

THE SWAN INN

Lamberhurst Down, Lamberhurst.
Tel: (0892) 890200

One of the most charming and unspoilt inns in the whole of this part of the county, The Swan at Lamberhurst is pretty as a picture. The inn is next to the famed Lamberhurst vineyards, and is set in the heart of the weald of Kent. Here is home-cooking at its very best, featuring local fruit and vegetables, grown in the garden of England, locally caught trout, game (in season) and fresh salads. At lunchtime a wide variety of home-made traditional dishes are offered, with snacks and daily specials from the blackboard. The ploughman's are reputedly the best in the south of England. In the evening a large à la carte is offered, consisting of Scotch rump steaks, fillet steaks, Dover soles, supreme of chicken Anton, duck breast Cointreau and lots of other exciting dishes. Visitors are certain not to be disappointed. A fine beer garden to enjoy in summer, a haven of warmth and welcome inside in autumn and winter.

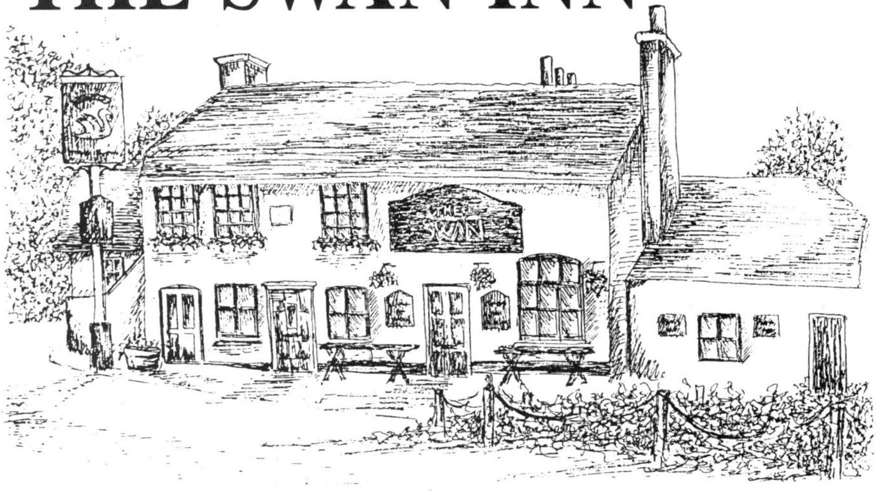

THE ROSE & CROWN

High Street, Brenchley.
Tel: (089 272) 2107

The first licence was granted 'for sale of ales and cider, but not on the Sabbath' in 1745, and this lovely inn has been looking after the needs of the traveller ever since. More than this, here is an inn that has built up an enviable reputation for food, and is now in the most capable and imaginative hands of owners Rowley Hill and Alison Jones, whose personal touch is evident in every aspect of the inn. Twelve fine bedrooms, all *en suite* with colour televisions, direct dial telephones, some with four-poster beds and one with a jacuzzi – an ideal honeymoon suite. The restaurant menu changes regularly, with examples of starters and main courses including seafood gratin (prawns, scallops and mussels in white wine and cheese sauce), baked avocado with prawns in a tomato sauce, warm smoked turkey and Waldorf salad, then pheasant in red wine or shark steaks in a basil and cream sauce.

Just off the B2160, near Tonbridge

Dinner

Closed for food Monday night

Dinner £14.95
Sunday lunch £6.95
Lunch from £2.50 – £6
House wine from £5.50 – £30 per bottle

Gourmet evenings
Private parties and conferences

12 bedrooms ***en suite***

Access, Visa, Amex, Diner's Club

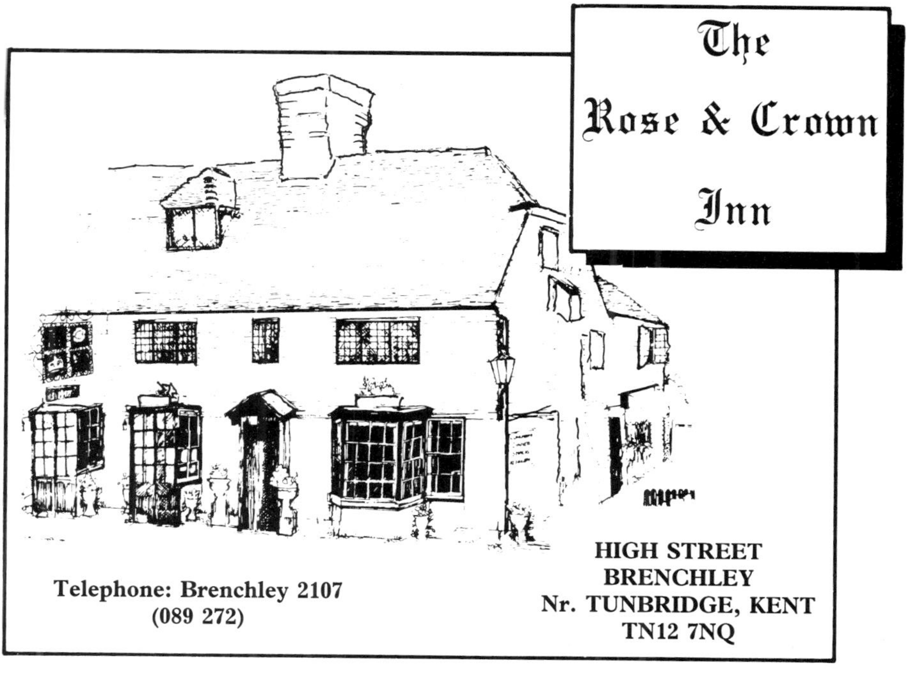

THE GEORGE

VOTE FOR THE

WHERE TO EAT

We want you to help us find the Kent Restaurant of the Year, to be featured in the next edition of Where to Eat.

During the compilation of the next edition, we will be asking the region's caterers for their choice as the best eating place. We would, however, like you – the people who eat out regularly – to take part as well.

A form is provided below for you to tell us where you consider to be the best eating place in the area. It could be an establishment featured in this guide, or a recommendation of your own. You can nominate a formal restaurant, a country inn, a town pub, a wine bar/bistro or even a coffee ship or tearoom.

Everyone who submits a nomination will receive a complimentary copy of next year's guide.

My choice for Restaurant of the Year is

____

at ______________________________________

Name ____________________________________

Address __________________________________

Please send your votes to:

Restaurant of the Year,
Where to Eat in Kent,
Kingsclere Publications Ltd.,
2 Highfield Avenue,
Newbury, Berkshire, RG14 5DS

CHEF'S CHOICE

In each of our regional **Where to Eat** guides, we ask an experienced chef, well-respected in the area, to prepare one of his favourite menus.

Robert Sloan

Robert Sloan, who has been running The Royal Wells Inn with his brother David for the past 21 years, spent four years at Ealing Hotel and Catering College, studying Hotel Management.

His interest in cooking blossomed when helping his father set up the hotel in 1967. He immediately took to cooking and developed the skills, the basics of which were learnt at Ealing, to produce menus of flair and imagination.

He doesn't fall into any particular style, but admits to preparing only the freshest food in a manner that he would enjoy sitting down to eat himself.

STARTER
Scallops in Puff Pastry

Sliced plump king scallops, served under puff pastry in the shell, with a fine julienne of vegetables and small mousselines of sole moistened with dry sherry and flavoured with dill. A crisp, dry Loire wine would partner this dish well.

WINE
Sancerre 1988, Guy Saget

SECOND COURSE
Navarin of Lamb

The proximity of the South Downs ensures the exellence of this simple, yet underrated, stew of leg of lamb and fresh baby vegetables. To complement the dish an underrated wine such as Romanian Pinot Noir.

WINE
Romanian Pinot Noir 'Classic' 1986, from the Dealul Mare region

MAIN COURSE
Breast of Duck with Russet Apples

Living on the doorstep of 'The Garden of England' gave rise to this dish. Breast of duck, stuffed with russet apples, sage and cinnamon, then roasted in butter, wine vinegar and sugar. The roasting juices then form the sauce with the addition of a jelly made from redcurrants. The complex tastes of this dish perfectly suit a quality Bordeaux.

WINE
Château la Gurgue, Margaux, 1987

DESSERT
Chestnut Ice-Cream

We began serving this simple dish one autumn after taking my dog for a walk over the common and returning with a bag full of chestnuts. Having dispensed with the laborious task of shelling the nuts, we made a subtle tasting ice-cream which is served in a crisp brandy snap basket on an anglais flavoured with chestnut and cherry brandy.

WINE
Château du Rolland, 1986

INDEX

ALPHABETICAL INDEX TO ESTABLISHMENTS

The Barn, Tunbridge Wells 6
The Bell, Smarden 47
The Brokers Arms, Tunbridge Wells 22
The Crown Inn at Finglesham, near Deal 38
The Dog and Bear Hotel, Lenham, near Maidstone 9
Eastwell Manor, Boughton Aluph, near Ashford 41
The Eight Bells, Tenterden 45
The Elephant's Head, Hook Green, Lamberhurst 54
Fleur de Lis, Brenzett, Romney Marsh 43
Gardner's Restaurant, Rolvenden 44
The George, Frant, near Tunbridge Wells 58
Giovanni's Whitstable 12
The Hengist, Aylesford, Maidstone 8
The Kennel Holt Country House Hotel, Cranbrook 53
The King's Arms, Headcorn 48
The King's Arms, Meopham 27
The King's Head Restaurant, Bessels Green, Sevenoaks 25
The Lord Raglan, Staplehurst 49
The Mad Chef's Bistro, Broadstairs 36
Marchesi, Broadstairs 13
The Marina Resort Hotel, Ramsgate 14
The Mount Edgcumbe House Hotel, Tunbridge Wells 5
The Place in Marden Restaurant, Marden 50
The Queen's Arms, Egerton Forstal, Ashford 42
The Queen's Head Hotel, Hawkhurst 16
The Rose & Crown, Brenchley 57
The Rose and Crown, Tonbridge 7
The Royal Albion Hotel, Broadstairs 35
The Royal Oak, Beneden 15
The Royal Oak, Upstreet, near Canterbury 34
The Royal Wells Inn, Tunbridge Wells 20
Sankey's Seafood Bar and Restaurant at the Gate, Tunbridge Wells 17
The Shant Hotel and Prince of Wales, East Sutton near Maidstone. 31
The Ship Inn and Smuggler's Restaurant, Teynham, near Sittingbourne . . 32

I

The Spa Hotel, Tunbridge Wells 18
The Spotted Dog, Penhurst 24
Soufflé, Bearsted, Maidstone 28
The Swan Hotel, Tunbridge Wells 21
The Swan Inn, Lamberhurst Down, Lamberhurst 56
Throwley House, Sheldwich, Faversham 11
Wallet's Court, St Margaret's at Cliffe 37
Weeks of Goudhurst 55
The White Hart, Brasted, Westerham 26
The Wife of Bath, Wye 39
Ye Mades Restaurant, Biddenden 46

I

ALPHABETICAL INDEX TO TOWNS AND VILLAGES

Aylesford 8
Bearsted 28
Benenden 15
Bessels Green 25
Biddenden 46
Boughton Aluph 41
Brasted 26
Brenchley 57
Brenzett 43
Broadstairs 13,35
Cranbrook 53
East Sutton 31
Egerton Forstal 42
Finglesham 38
Frant 58
Goudhurst 55
Hawkhurst 16
Headcorn 48
Hook Green 54
Lamberhurst Down 56
Lenham 9
Marden 50
Meopham Green 27
Penshurst 24
Ramsgate 14
Rolvenden 44
St Margaret's at Cliffe 37
Sheldwich 11
Smarden 47
Staplehurst 49
Tenterden 45
Teynham 32
Tonbridge 7
Tunbridge Wells 5,17
Upstreet 34
Whitstable 12
Wye 39